THE HITLERIAD

THE
HITLERIAD

A. M. KLEIN

The Poets of the Year — New Directions

New Direction Books are published by James Laughlin

New York Office — 67 West 44 — 18

THE HITLERIAD

I

Heil heavenly muse, since also thou must be
Like my song's theme, a sieg-heil'd deity,
Be with me now, but not as once, for song:
Not odes do I indite, indicting Wrong!
Be with me, for I fall from grace to sin,
Spurning this day thy proffered hippocrene,
To taste the poison'd lager of Berlin!

Happier would I be with other themes —
(Who rallies nightmares when he could have dreams?)
With other themes, and subjects more august—
Adolf I sing but only since I must.
I must! Shall I continue the sweet words
That praise the blossoming flowers, the blossoming birds,
While, afar off, I hear the stamping herds?
Shall I, within my ivory tower, sit
And play the solitaire of rhyme and wit,
While Indignation pounds upon the door,
And Pity sobs, until she sobs no more,
And, in the woods, there yelp the hounds of war?

I am the grandson of the prophets! I
Shall not seal lips against iniquity.
Let anger take me in its grasp; let hate,
Hatred of evil prompt me, and dictate!
And let the world see that swastika-stain,
That heart, where no blood is, but high octane,
That little brain —
So that once seen the freak be known again!

[5]

Oh, even as his truncheon'd crimes are wrought,
And while the spilt blood is still body-hot,
And even as his doom still seems in doubt,
Let deeds unspeakable be spoken out.
Wherefore, O Muse, I do invoke thy aid,
Not for the light and sweetness of the trade,
But seeing I draw a true bill of the Goth,
For the full fire of thy heavenly wrath!
Aid me, and in good time, for as I talk
The knave goes one step nearer to the dock;
And even as triumphant cannon boom
He marches on his victories—to doom!

II

See him, at last, the culprit twelve men damn.
Is this the face that launched the master-race
And burned the topless towers of Rotterdam?
Why, it's a face like any other face
Among a sea of faces in a mob—
A peasant's face, an agent's face, no face
At all, no face but vegetarian blob!
The skin's a skin on eggs and turnips fed,
The forehead villainous low, the eyes deepset—
The pervert big eyes of the thwarted bed—
And that mustache, the symbol of the clown
Made emperor, and playing imperial pranks—
Is this the mustache that brought Europe down,
And rolled it flat beneath a thousand tanks?

III

Judge not the man for his face
Out of Neanderthal!

[6]

'Tis true 'tis commonplace,
Mediocral,
But the evil of the race
Informs that skull!

You ask, is paragon'd
The Nordic in this thrall?
Why, chivalry's not found
In him at all!
And he's the beast not blond,
Nor is he tall.

His strength is as the strength
Of ten, and ten times ten;
For through him, magnified
Smallness comes to our ken—
The total bigness of
All little men.

IV

The dossier, then; the facts, the untampered text:
Let *this* world know him, ere he goes to the next!
Where was he born? (Born is the word that I
Use, seeing *littered* is not poesy.)
Where was he born? In Braunau at the Inn—
And Austria paid for that original sin!—
Born to a father, old and over-wined
Who had he slept one night, had saved mankind!
At first hight Shicklgruber—'what a name
To herald through the mighty trump of fame'—
Heil Schicklgruber! Schicklgruber, heil!
Methinks this lacks the true imperial style,

And certainly no poet's nor mob's tongue
Could shake from shekel-shackle-gruber—song!
The gods are kind. His father changed his name,
And saved, at least the Shicklgrubers' shame.
Soon he removed to Linz. Now, note this well,
This was the town where Rilke wove his spell,
Where Rilke dreamed the beautiful and good—
And on this *boden*, Hitler dreamed of *blut!*
His teachers have since died; and fortunate they
Who else had died ten deaths to see the day
The dunce of the corner corner better men,
And great wealth his who could not count to ten!
Doctrine he spurned, and scholarship despised:
Let others win the palms so meanly prized—
The teacher's apple and the fiat lux—
Sheepskin for sheep, and for the bookworm books.
Let others learn to love their fellowmen;
He had no fellow, neither now, nor then.
Let others learn to love their neighbours. He
Hated his father and all Linz-ery
(Forgive the young: he'd see his hate untwined
To take in, generously, all humankind.)
Wherefore, uncouth, untutored, unconcerned,
He left his school most thoroughly unlearned,
Fit for the plough—before it, not behind!—
And as time proved, the premier German mind!

V

But did he not in art show promise, such
As to forgive, if not all ignorance, much?
He did; the first of many promises
Still unfulfilled, most tolerable, this:

He drew a line, it was not crooked, so
He thought that he was Michelangelo!
Yet is it true that in due time, he would
Incarnadine him murals with much blood;
To Europe's marbled treasures adding his
Ruins out-ruining Acropolis;
Yes, with a continent for easel, he
Would yet show vicious virtuosity,
Would yet achieve the opus of his dream,
The classic painting, masterpiece supreme:
The Reich's *Last Supper* (out of stolen pots)
With quislings six, and six iscariots!

Meanwhile he dreamed, and dreaming saw himself
Rich and esteemed on many a library shelf,
In many paintings hanging from a wall,
(This hanging theme, is it prophetical?)
And *Hitler fecit, pinxit Hitler* was
The only Latin of his final class.
He comes before his betters to stand test:
Is this an artist, for he is ill-dressed?
Is he to paint, because he cannot write?
We believe his linens would look better—white!
And for the first time Adolf's judged aright.

VI

Here stutters biography.   The scribes conflict
In qualifying Vienna's derelict:
Was he a bricklayer, as some aver,
A paperhanger, or a carpenter?
The witnesses ignore.

It seems, in any case, — symbolic thing! —
He always worked on scaffolding.
Some others say—on oath—he had no trade,
Blame his survival on the public aid.
He slept, they say, in flophouses; he wore
Castoff; he ate handouts at the door;
('Tis no disgrace. Disgraceful only is
Ignoring in others one's own miseries.)
He fed on alms, these say. 'Twas Jewish food.
Hate knows no firmer ground than gratitude.

VII

And then there came—blow, trumpets; drummers, drum!—
The apocalypse, the pandemonium,
The war the Kaiser from his shrivelled hand
Let fall upon the European land.
Mark well, O men, the manner of our man:
He who not once in his entire life-span
Was either by sympathy or sorrow swept,
Heard of the carnage imminent—and wept!
He wept—but let us his own words employ:
"I fell on my knees, I wept, I wept for joy!"

Now this was the stuff of which a soldier's made!
But after four years, where is Adolf's braid?
Where are his medals? His promotions, where?
He had none; could it be he'd failed to dare?
Or could it be the brave of the front-line
Too often showed the salient his spine,
And chose too often duties, unsung, drear—
But safe—"to bring dispatches to the rear"?
O could it be that this was, after all,

How Adolf humbly stayed a corporal?
Alas, that then the untaught General Staff
Knew *intuition* as an epitaph,
And did not, as in later times, bestow
On this non-sense its generalissimo!

VIII

Why, even in his private little war,
His march on Munich, when for the first time
This painter showed his phobia of red,
It was old Ludendorff, the warrior,
Still battling Foch, but now in pantomime,
Who marched breast forward, while—while Adolf fled,
Fled, with the fleeing of his own brave words,
Fled, fell on his face, and not upon his spear,
Got up, and fled, a rabbit to its hutch.
Such was the hero, flashing others' swords!
Such was the leader, leading bouts with beer!
Such was the puttering-out of the Great Putsch!

IX

Let it be said of Hitler, then, that he
Had courage, when he had a guarantee;
He risked, when primed assurance smiled; he dared
When the positions had been well-prepared.
He sought the German power—but no haste:
The dotard Hindenburg would see him placed.
He marched across the Rhine; yet it was plain
A bullet would have marched him back again.

He coveted the Czech-land; yet he waited
Until that prize was generously donated.
Circumspect, cautious, of an humble air—
Until he found he could afford to dare.
Then, summoning the pensioned warriors,
Then, even then, he followed his true course,
Mounting no charger, but a Trojan horse!

X

So, you may say, he was a miracle
Of bold persuasion and of iron will—
And sure he needs no courage who has skill!
What skill? And what persuasion? Skill to use
Hatred as bomb, and rhetoric as fuse?
Persuasion to persuade the Swabian mind
It was the unwhipped cream of humankind?
A bag of tricks, a mountebank's recipes,
Fit only for the half-mentalities
By birth and training sedulously bred
To swap, for circuses, their daily bread.
Consider with what petty bribes these were
Perverted from both Kant's and Goethe's lore,
Pure Reason bartering for Force impure,
And their Faust-soul betraying for a whore!
Consider for what baubles they sold out:
The shoddy uniform; the chorus'd shout;
The bonfired books; the robot-like salutes;
The ever-marching military boots!
These, such as these, no genius, but mere quack
Could soon reduce from people to a claque,
And bid them be, enamoured and enticed,
Of crooked cross re-crucifying Christ!

XI

Go to *Mein Kampf* if you would know his trade,
And there learn how a people is unmade,
And how, with mocking pantomime,
The tyrants on its ruins climb.
There learn the rules,
(Transparent unto all, save fools)
There take the lessons from the literate boors
And learn to lead the lofty-destined Reich—
Or Barnum-Bailey tours!
Learn it from Adolf's very prosiness,
Indited by his fellow-convict, Hess,
(Though adept at the demagogic yell,
It is averred that Adolf could not spell)
Learn it from him, who, east, west, north and south,
Excelled in the loud bigness of his Mouth!

Learn
How with the double-jointed rhetoric
He turned men's minds—(and stomachs)—and the trick;
Hear him reveal the charlatan's technique:
The prearranged ad-libs, the advised shriek,
The spontaneities prepared, the stance
Best suited for prophetic eloquence,
The iterated and ecstatic prose,
And above all, the pose, the Wagnerian pose!
And hear him brief his wisdom, brashly smooth:
"The lie, if oft repeated, is the truth!"

Read, marvelling, the slogans that did foil
The Hun intelligence; Blood, Honour, Soil:
The worship of the blood, in Arians veined,
And in all others preferably uncontained;

[13]

The practice of an Honour, modified
By the dear temperature of one's own hide;
And as for Soil, a simple ratio:
Nazis above, all others deep below!

Add then, the insured craft with which he chose
The chosen people for his choicest prose:
Here was a scapegoat to his measure made,
Big enough to inform his wild tirade
And too small to return its foe his due:
The strange ubiquitous Jew!

When could one find a better scapegoat than
The bearded Hebrew cosmopolitan,
Than this the Israelite, not far to seek,
Who was at once an alien, and weak?
Is it the rich who rouse the tribune's ire?
Some Jews are rich, and can well feed his fire.
Is it the poor, the indigent radical?
Judaea's destitution is not small.
The Jew's unsocial—he will not join in
The civic hubbub, the political din,
And also he's too forward; everywhere
Smell his ambitious presence in the air!
Pietist, he pollutes with his old creed
The pagan vigour of the German breed;
And at the same time lifts the mystic mist
From off the German mind—the atheist!
All evil from this Marxian plutocrat:
The Weimar laws, and the Versailles diktat,
The lowered standards and the rising costs,
Inflation and heat-waves, taxes and sharp frosts,
All, all achieved by the Semitic hosts.

The theorem did not matter, nor its flaws—
Sufficient to sneer "Jew" to win applause,
Yelp "Jude," and await the frenzied jeers—
And thus assure the Reich its thousand years!

So did he still the German hunger with
The ever-novel but right ancient myth,
And taught his people first to heil and hoot,
Then legislate, then doom, then persecute,
Visiting even on the blondest Jew
The crime his great-great-great-grandmother knew!

Such his persuasion, and — the authentic curse —
Such the too-soon persuaded Berliners.
(Observe the method in this madness, since
The Jew being beaten, the world did not wince,
The vogue was shown, by flesh-barometer,
He could persist, yet no great risk incur.)

XII

Yet not alone
Did Hitler do the deeds for which he must atone!
Henchmen he had,
Spirits and genii whom he did evoke
Out of the bottled Herren-volk,
Frustrated men, who'd tried all things, and failed,
And then determined to be jailed, or hailed!
Herr Goebbels such a one —
Club-footed, rat-faced, halitotic, the
Brave Nordic ideal, a contrario!
A kept man; eloquent, a Ph.D;
Carried no gun, forsooth; a radio
Lethal enough for him, shouting its lies,

Exploding lebensraum and libido;
Subtle in puncturing all human foibles
Saving his own, prolific in alibis—
Goebbels.

And such that other, Rosenberg,
The penman of the mob; had written books;
Corrected Adolf's grammar; could devise
Seventy reasons for atrocities;
Scorned pity; credited with stabbing hooks
Into the too-compassionate Christian crux;
Concocted, weekly, blood-philosophies,
To genuflect non-Arians to their knees;
Was daft about his twentieth-century spooks;
Herr Rosenberg, burdened with double shame:
A Baltic birth, and a Semitic name.

Nor was he absent, that ubiquity,
Goering, the arsonist, who loved disguise—
A uniform for every pantomime,
Including asbestos for the Reichstag crime—
Goering distinguished, mainly, by his size,
By the great girth's unrationed symmetries,
Ridiculous, in ersatz-land, sublime!
There was geheimrat who was not geheim!
Big in his own, and other people's eyes!
Loved hunting, preferably biped quarry;
Loved art, if stolen; loved imported grub;
Addicted to the narcotic and the gory;
Bore weapons (daggers); lead a lion-cub;
And thought that full-face photos spread his glory.
(There is, of course, no profile to a tub.)

[16]

Nor yet was overlooked the fashion-plate:
Be not deceived by the manners of this fop,
His hat and gloves, his apathetic heils.
This was no dandy, but a man of wiles,
The double-swasticrossing Ribbentrop.
Think him not milksop, no, nor champagne-sop.
His morning coat was cut to the latest styles
Of armour-plate; he was the villain who smiles,
And pours the cocktails with the poison-drop.
He was the fingerman who spied the job;
The Cliveden layout was his tour-de-force,
And it was he contacted the Vichy mob,
And he who fed oats to the Trojan horse,
'Twas he, the master of the slick hobnob,
Who put in protocol the Nazi curse!

XIII

And other lesser fry there were
Who joined the Nazi exchequer,
Careerists who sought living-space
Upon the body of their race,
Each coming forward, for a price,
To sell his own especial vice:
Von Papen, spy and diplomat,
Hiding low cunning in high hat,
Giving his masters fealty
As long as they held mastery,
Reliable, whate'er might happen
To serve the good of Herr Von Papen!

And Himmler, Heinrich, mild and meek,
Most studious of the human shriek,

Inquisitive about the extent
To which men could take punishment,
Already planning for the foe
The order of the Gestapo,
Already practising to bowl
With all the heads that needs must roll,
Already forging chains and gyves
For the long night of the long knives,
Himmler, most self-effacing, and
Effacing others with Kultur's impartial hand.

Oily, obscene, fat as a hog,
The thick scourge of the synagogue,
The loutish uncouth pedagogue,
Streicher, brings up his hefty rear,
Among his bandit peers, a peer —
Meet now, the brothel-keeper for
The votaries of racial lore,
Who procured, by his journal's traffic
The titillation pornographic,
The lewd urge, the concupiscent thrill
By which he proved him human still.

He also stood, with beckoning claw
Holding uncandid camera—
The fawning Hoffman, who dared give
The Fuehrer his sole negative;
And he, hook-nosed, was also there,
The learnéd doctor Haushofer,
Expanding Hitler's empery
By dint of pure cartography:
The soldiers pluck what his school picks—
The art is geopolitics.

Nor should one fail to speak to-day
Of the besotted Robert Ley
Since drunken underneath a table
To speak himself he is unable;
Nor yet forget—alack-a-day,
Volatile Hess who flew away.

O what a crew unto their leader like!
As master mongrel, so each crawling tike,
And all the saviours of the German Reich!

XIV

Aye, were not others at that honeymoon,
Herr Strasser and his strange gregorian tune,
And Captain Roehm, ever in love with youth,
Best man among the paladins of truth?
Where are they now?
These knights reproachable but without fear?
O where is Shleicher's intellectual brow?
Why does not Heines, stalwart, reappear?
Where are the crows of yesteryear?

Departed, gentlemen, but without dirge.
The gallant Fuehrer had to have his purge;
These worthies, therefore, came to bitter ends:
They'd sinned the supreme sin—they were his friends!

XV

Yet not by their sole aid did Adolf rise,
His greatest help came from his enemies:
The eye-glass'd Junker looking down
Upon the upstart corporal clown;

The simple Social Democrat;
The Catholic, and concordat;
The too-shrewd plutocratic vons
Thyssen, Hugenberg and sons;
The dialectic theorist who saw the ever-thickening mist
And cheered, in hope that soon therefrom
The light, hegelian, would come;
And even Hindenburg, who in alarm,
Sold a republic for a private farm!

Each in his fashion, and for personal sake
Led Germany to Hitler's stake.
Yes, let it be told, let it be written down
How even from afar
There came the aid that burned the Republic brown;
Let it be told
How gold tycoon, how monied czar,
Reaction black, and Interest, dirty-grey
Trembled before the rumour of that plot
Plotting for Europe its Muscovian day,
And trembling, dropped more coin into the Nazi pot!

Let us not name the names, but let us speak
Only about munition'd dividends,
Of markets rising to an envied peak,
Of rubber's conscienceless elastic ends,
Of timely trains by fascists always mann'd,
And of umbrellas, which, alas, did leak.
Those who have memory will understand.

XVI

Who are those thousands in the goose-step march?
Athletes, said Papen, sly and arch.

Whose are those planes that through the ether race?
Commerce, said Goering, with cherubic face.
The tanks that still keep coming, on and on?
Said innocent Ley: The *Volkswagon.*
And all those lovely gases, what are they?
Said Goebbels: *Cure-alls for a better day.*

Within the chancelleries, the diplomats
Chuckled and winked behind their polished hats;
And Downing Street announced from Number Ten
The balance of power balanced once again.

XVII

There were—the decade's grace—who saw
This moulting of the moral law,
Who cried against the knaveries
Designed to please and to appease,
And such an one was he who stood
Late and alone against the flood,
The man who hated sham and cant,
Unfortunately brilliant,
Churchill, who kept our world extant!

Across the seas, still doomed to wait,
Man's conscience-made-articulate,
Roosevelt sent forth his biblic words
As he would yet send forth, for vengeance
The steel leviathans, the flaming swords,
The swift seraphic engines!

Ah, he who might have led great France
Against the brazen countenance,
Was gone from twilight into night —
The Tiger, ever-burning bright!

XVIII

But was there not, to cope with this intrigue—
To keep the peace—the wise Wilsonian league?
The League of Nations—what a hope was there,
Fled with the years, vanished in spoken air!
It could have had no other fate. Alas,
Who looked, could long have seen it in the glass:
The kisses blown with weak asthmatic breath
By old men gesturing themselves to death.
Were these the men to put teeth in the law,
Who had no tooth in their collective jaw?
Were these the men that would the peace maintain
Themselves upholding only with a cane?
Could these look in the future, who could not
See without specs, and those, at home, forgot?
Most miserable world which had to lean
Upon the dotards of this dying scene!

While such as these, then, guard the public weal
And safety totters, and security
Goes palsied, doddering and down-at-heel,
While Senex drones, and all Geneva snores,
He'd be no burglar, who in such event
Did not bethink him of his burglary,
To try his key in all the tempting doors!

And Hitler read his opportunity!

XIX

How blind these were, he thought, who did not see
The new excalibur that rose in air
That certain weapon of short victory,
Which using, even the unrash might dare

[22]

The great assault, the sudden lightning thrust!
Before this thing, defenses could not score,
And pacts were sand, and maginot were dust—
This Stuka of the fourth-dimensional war!
Let then, the old men, therefore, rack their wits,
Magniloquizing their paralysis
As if it were a tactic of Clausevitz.
From hidden hangars and fake factories
Would soon emerge the weapons of the blitz!
Then would there be, old men, a peace, the peace
That passeth boundaries!

XX

Now, the career he built on such foundations
With allies, passive, active, such as these
Is black and public on the garb of nations.
It has no secrecies.
Is there a wickedness this wicked man
Did not accomplish? An iniquity
That he did not decree?
A crime that was not indexed in his plan?
He did encompass all
The high crimes and the misdemeanours low,
Enormous, diabolical,
Lavish of suffering, and of woe
Beyond recall.

I shall not here complain that he did not
Know decency, or love, or honour, or
The other virtues surplus to the codes:
They were beyond his thought,
Here was a land his spies did not explore—
Uncharted were these roads.

But Law, uncommentaried and unburden'd Law,
The child-eye choosing between right and wrong,
The manly option made against the beast,
That, by the man so high above the throng,
That might have been expected,
That, at least!
At least! That little least was more
Than he could suffer, who despised
The norms that only weak men prized—
Not Pity, cloth by cripple spun,
Not Justice—blind—he put out both her eyes,
Nor Culture, here he cocked his gun,
Nor Worth, nor yet Humanity effete,
The weakling's meat!

Wherefore, in lieu of the illumined law
He ushered in, the better for his deeds,
The burglar's darkness and the murderer's fog.
He tore the statutes; he abjured the creeds;
He stamped on the Decalogue!

He coveted.
O what did this much-shrivelled little soul
Not covet, not lust after? Everything
That was not his:
The painter's brush, a purer genesis,
The fame of letters not won by himself,
Bismarckian role,
Power and place and pelf.

But had he merely coveted, merely bayed
At the unreachable reaches of the distant moon,

Out of his thwarting, out of hope delayed
He would have perished soon,
Heart-broken, foiled, his wrist-veins cut—
But
He also stole. He was a thief. He stole.
Even the credos of his sloganry
He piecemeal filched to make a patchwork whole.
(Forgiveable—a petty larceny!)
His depredations rose.
He robbed the rich; impartial, robbed the dole.
The folk he loved, he taxed; and those he hated
He confiscated.
The poor man for his pension-pennies sobbed.
The church he also held up for its toll.
The house of God was robbed.

Fed thus with native quarry, flesh and gore
He licked his whiskers, crouched, then stalked for more.

XXII

See, on historic film his crimes deployed,
Felonies flickering from celluloid!
And through the planes' sharp retina, behold
His victims, and their plight,
The beaten, and the ambushed, and the sold!

Austria, gay and bright and musical
Receiving in the silenced hall
The mud-bespattered guest;
And brave Bohemia—Honour's epitaph—
Broken in half,
Half blackmailed, plundered of the rest.

[25]

(Watch for the montage of accomplishd guile:
As Skoda skids, the four smug men will smile.)

The scenes now change, but madness knows no halt.
Norway is sacked, and Poland's sown with salt
Explosive! Holland also visited,
　　Whose dykes and Dutchmen bled.

(Montage again: the camera goes berserk
With vertical flame and towers diagonal;
Then rests to show the generals; they smirk.)

Closeup. The fascist and his rods
Flogging the Jugoslavian fading out
To Greece, her freemen broken, like her gods.

Roofs; and the Eiffel Tower's prominence—
France!
Bereft of Buonaparte
Her sated mirrors shattered, and her heart.
France, that too soon, too humble, did descend
From brightness to the dark,
Bereft of Joan of Arc,
Upon an evil day on evil hours come.
Within her conquered hall
Domremy voice is dumb.
The lesser corporal
Over prostrated France
Mimics with carpet-fretting feet
Napoleonic stance!

Look west, and see the towers of London-town
Declining, battered, but not battered down—
The burglar mounted, but he came too late:

He broke, but did not enter.
Look east, the Russian lifts avenging hands,
Waylaid, assaulted, wounded—he still stands
By dint of that unthawed triumvirate;
Cold steel, and Stalin cool, and icy Winter!

XXIII

As footnote to the headlined Terror, know
His ally fared no better than his foe.
War was a science; treaties were an art.
Wherefore, with artful pacts, he pushed the free
Contracting the parties of the second part
Through slow contraction to nihility.
Met, plenipotent — farewelled, impotent,
They came as sovereigns, and as servants went.
He made of Magyarland a state in fee,
A German province out of Italy,
A dairy out of Denmark, and
An oil-well of Roumanian land.

And are these methods banned?
Where treaties could avail, why use the rod?
Why seek by force, what could be got by fraud?
He'd even make a ten-year truce with God!
To bear false witness was no crime.   Wherefore
Upon his blood-and-soiled honour swore
He longed for peace. Was believed. And then
    prepared for war.

XXIV

Nor did he merely wage his war on Man.
Against the Lord he raised his brazen brow,
Blasphemed His name, His works, contemned His plan,

Himself a god announced, and bade men bow
Down to his image, and its feet of clay!
God's places of true worship were laid low,

And idols on the high places held their sway;
Astrologers were prophets in the land,
And mad philosophers rose to inveigh

Against the diktat of the Lord's command.
Iniquity espoused, and evil wived,
Kindliness, pity, brother-love, were banned.

The creed of the Black Forest was revived,
And ceased the ancient pieties for men.
Of manliness and godliness deprived,

The pagan, named for beasts, was born again.
The holy days were gone. The Sabbath creed
Unfit for slaves, superfluous to his reign,

Stood unobserved. The nine-month-littered breed
Traduced their parents to the Gestapo;
Adulterous, the stud-men spawned their seed.

The Madman named the Lord his personal foe.
And chained the bearers of His sacred word.
This is the sign, he shrilled: *In hoc vinco!*

He raised aloft the blood-stained sword;
Upon the square the heathen horde
Roared.

XXV

But not with human arrogance come I
To plead our Maker's cause, and make His cause

The mighty measure of my feeble words.
Himself, in His good time, the Lord of Hosts,
The slowness of His anger moved at last,
And His longsuffering at last forespent
Will rise, will shine, will stretch forth His right hand
And smite them down, the open impious mouth,
The tongue blaspheming, silenced, in the dust!

I come now rather as a man to men,
Seeking the justice for that voice which cries
Out of the ground, the voice of our brothers' blood!
That blood will not be still again,
Those bones unblessed will still arise,
Yes, and those living spectres, of the mind unhinged,
Will still beat at our padded memory, until
Their fate has been avenged!

XXVI

Let them come forth, those witnesses who stand
Beyond the taunt of perjury, those ghosts
In wagons sealed in a forgotten land,
Murdered; those phantoms the war-tidings boast,
Those skeletons still charred with the gestapo brand!

Let them come forth and speak, who lost their speech
Before the midnight gun-butt on the door,
The men made dumb with their last voiceless screech
In ghetto-yard, and on the Dachau floor —
Let them accuse now, who did once in vain beseech!

Summon them, bailiff of the dead, the ghosts
Who once were brave men stood against a wall,
Summon them, all the exsanguinated hosts,

[29]

Hero and martyr, liquidated; call,
Call forth the witnesses, the uninterred ghosts,

And let them speak. And let the dead attest
Their murder and its manner and its cause —
From shattered jaw, from perforated breast
Speak out their mauling at the bestial claws.
Speak out, or neither we, nor they, again know rest.

Let them in all their thousands speak the shame
Visited on them, and the ignoble death,
The nameless ones, and those of a great fame:
With wounded whisper and with broken breath
Speaking the things unspeakable, and the
    unspeakable name!

Then from such evidence, such witnessing,
Surely the anger of the world will burst,
Surely the wrath of nations will outfling
Against this culprit, multitude-accursed
Doom indexed by the black gloves of their reckoning!

Thief, perjurer, blasphemer, murderer,
Let him be blotted out, and all his crew.
Efface the evil; let it be no more.
Let the abomination cease; and through
Implacable Justice let emerge the world, clean, new!

Bold malefaction brought at last to bay!
Avenged the martyrs! Mankind truly purged!

Returned at last the spectres to their clay!
And over the green earth, at last emerged,
After the cock-crow of the guns, the cloudless day!

XXVII

And on that day as the unrighteous pass,
Unrighteousness will pass away, and men
Will see once more, as when their vision was
Illumined by the lightning strokes the ten—
Gesturing Truth ungagged will speak again,
And Man will don his godliness once more—
Then from four corners of the earth will sing
The sons of heaven, the bright freedoms four;
The field will glow again with harvesting,
And glow with argosies the deep; again
Will frolic in the ether, sunlight-blue'd—
Not the grim vulture of the brood
Its talons dripping blood,
But the bright friendly somersaulting plane
Writing against the sky
So all may read on high
Man loyal to his human brotherhood,
To human brotherhood, and to the godly reign!

N · D

PRINTED FOR NEW DIRECTIONS
BY SAMUEL MARCUS PRESS, CAMBRIDGE, MASSACHUSETTS

S · M

EARLIER TITLES IN "THE POETS OF THE YEAR" SERIES

1941

"Poems" by F. T. Prince
"The End of a Decade" by Harry Brown
"The Broken Span" by William Carlos Williams
"The Paradox in the Circle" by Theodore Spencer
"Shenandoah," a verse play by Delmore Schwartz
"More Poems from the Palatine Anthology" by Dudley Fitts
"A Letter from the Country & Other Poems" by Howard Baker
"Poems from The Book of Hours" by Rainer Maria Rilke
"Poems on Several Occasions" by Josephine Miles
"Some Poems & a Devotion" of John Donne
"Selected Poems" of John Wheelwright
"The Dry Season" by Malcolm Cowley

1942

"Poems" by John Berryman
"Some Poems" of Robert Herrick
"If There is Time" by Hildegarde Flanner
"The Lincoln Lyrics" by John Malcolm Brinnin
"The Sword on the Table" by Winfield Townley Scott
"Eleven Poems on the Same Theme" by Robert Penn Warren
"The Mirror of Baudelaire" edited by Charles Henri Ford
"Some Odes of Pindar" translated by Richmond Lattimore
"Our Lady Peace & Other War Poems" by Mark Van Doren
"The Teeth of the Lion" by Kenneth Patchen
"Selected Poems" by Carl Rakosi
"A Wreath of Christmas Poems"